101 Things I Learned in Law School

Other books in the 101 Things I Learned® series

101 Things I Learned® in Law School

Vibeke Norgaard Martin with Matthew Frederick

THREE RIVERS PRESS

NEW YORK

Copyright © 2013, 2019 by Matthew Frederick

All rights reserved.
Published in the United States by Three Rivers Press, an imprint of
the Crown Publishing Group, a division of Penguin Random House LLC, New York.
crownpublishing.com

Three Rivers Press and the Tugboat design are registered trademarks of
Penguin Random House LLC.

101 Things I Learned is a registered trademark of Matthew Frederick

Originally published in the United States in a slightly different form by
Grand Central Publishing, a division of Hachette Book Group, in 2013.

Library of Congress Cataloging-in-Publication Data is available upon request.

ISBN 978-1-5247-6202-5
Ebook ISBN 978-1-5247-6203-2

Printed in China

Illustrations by Matthew Frederick
Cover illustration by Matthew Frederick

10 9 8 7 6 5 4 3

First Three Rivers Press Edition

Author's Note

While this book was being written, a prominent public official was charged with sexually assaulting a chambermaid in his hotel room. The official claimed the maid had initiated the encounter. A famous defense lawyer, in presenting a mock closing argument to a trial advocacy class at Harvard Law School, attacked the defense's position. He suggested showing the jury a photograph of a naked, slightly overweight, and hunched 62-year-old man. The defense, the lawyer argued, would like the court to believe that the attractive 32-year-old maid set her eyes upon the defendant and "simply couldn't control herself."

The defense lawyer was using an old truth we lawyers know but do not pay enough attention to: a picture is worth a thousand words. But lawyers are word people. Take words away from us, and you take away our most important tool. We need words to argue, parse, and issue nuanced interpretations of complex legal concepts. But images should not be ignored, for they often provide access to concepts that words alone cannot impart with the same impact and economy.

For this reason and others, I jumped at the opportunity to create an illustrated introductory book on the law. When I was a beginning law student, I often felt frozen by the feeling that I knew nothing. Other students seemed to know much more than I did. They bandied about terms I didn't understand and projected a confidence I lacked. Often, I found myself wanting to chuck it all and do something else. I recall telling a fellow student that I wished I had followed my earlier dream to become a veterinarian, even though it might have meant putting puppies to sleep.

When I later started working at a large law firm, I came to realize that there is a certain amount of posturing in the field. Law is a sink-or-swim environment, and posturing is a way of intimidating those who are not inclined to fake their knowledge. But the likelihood, I have learned, is that the superconfident partner, professor, or law student may be as confused and intimidated by the law as I was. This book is for them, and for anyone else looking for a starting point to explore the complex questions of the law—and who would prefer not to wade through 101,000 words.

Vibeke Norgaard Martin

Acknowledgments

From Vibeke

Thanks to Dale Barnes, Michael Bowen, Susanne Caballero, Mike Clough, Ellen Gilmore, Ben Goldstone, Peter Jaszi, Ian Martin, Joe Mastro, Daniel Meyers, Amy Roach, and Bob Sims.

From Matt

Thanks to Karen Andrews, Tricia Boczkowski, Erik Bodenhofer, Sorche Fairbank, Laura Hankin, Dorothy Heyl, Matt Inman, Conrad Kickert, Amanda Patten, Angeline Rodriguez, Molly Stern, and Bruce Yandle.

Year 1
scare you to death

Year 2
work you to death

Year 3
bore you to death

A common characterization of law school

Law school doesn't teach laws.

One attends law school to learn how to think like a lawyer, not to memorize laws.
Laws change; how they are properly analyzed does not.

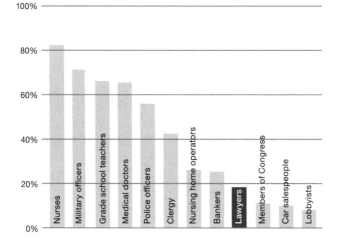

Percentage of citizens rating honesty and ethical standards of professionals as "very high" to "high"
Gallup, 2017

Honesty and truthfulness are different things.

Being honest means not telling lies. Being truthful means making known the full truth of a matter. Counsel may not lie to the court, but has no obligation to present a client's whole story.

A lawyer is a contextualist.

con·tex·tu·al·ist / kän–TEKS–chü–ə–list / *n.* (*pl.* **–ists**): a person who believes that the full meaning of a thing is not inherent in that thing, but depends on its relationship to other things.

Esquire

a lawyer;
traditionally
a member
of the landed
gentry

Attorney

anyone legally
empowered to
represent another,
e.g., with "power
of attorney"

Lawyer

one who is
formally a
member of
the legal
profession

Solicitor

(outside U.S.)
performs legal
work for clients
outside of
a trial

Barrister

(outside U.S.)
a specialist in
courtroom
advocacy; usually
hired by a solicitor

You're not a lawyer until you pass the bar.

The **bar** may refer to the entire legal profession, a formal portion of it, or the bar exam itself. Each state court system, the federal court system, and the U.S. Supreme Court is a separate bar with its own standards of admission and practice.

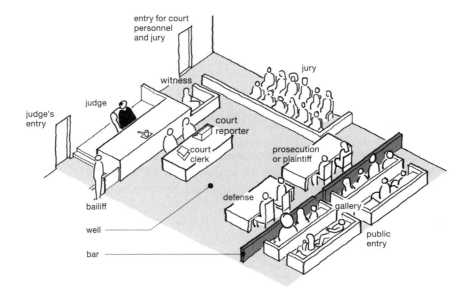

entry for court
personnel
and jury

jury

witness

judge

court
reporter

judge's
entry

court
clerk

prosecution
or plaintiff

bailiff

defense

gallery

well

public
entry

bar

You can't pass the bar until you're a lawyer.

A courtroom is divided into two parts by a railing or similar barrier called the **bar**. Only lawyers and their clients, when accompanied by their lawyer, may traverse it. The use of *bar* to refer to the legal profession as a whole derives from the tradition of barring nonparticipants from the trial area of the courtroom.

Common law

Civil law

In global context

Civil law

Criminal law

Within common law context

There are two ways to be civil.

In the global context, civil law and common law are the two primary legal systems. In **civil law nations,** the main source of law is legislation. In **common law nations,** new law—called case law—can also be created by the court through the decisions it makes in specific cases.

Within a common law system, civil law is concerned with noncriminal matters—for instance wrongs, or torts, committed by individuals, businesses, and institutions against each other. Criminal law is concerned with wrongs committed by individuals against society.

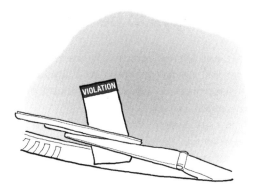

"Adversarial" isn't necessarily bad.

Most common law legal systems are **adversarial:** two sides, typically represented by expert advocates, argue their positions to the court. The judge does not directly investigate the case, and usually questions witnesses only to clarify confusing testimony.

In an **inquisitorial procedure,** a judge or group of judges directly investigates a case and questions litigants. Civil law nations typically employ inquisitorial procedures, while common-law nations tend to use them only for minor court disputes, such as traffic tickets and small claims.

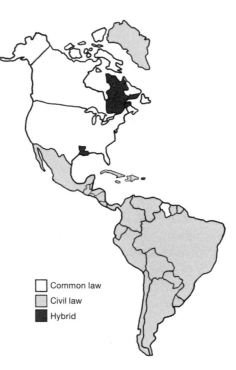

Common law

Civil law

Hybrid

All U.S. states, except Louisiana, have a primary heritage in English law.

Common law system

origin in 12th-century England

typical in English-speaking countries and former British colonies

adversarial

a court decision may become law that must be honored in subsequent cases

generally predictable, but adaptable

Civil law system

origin in Holy Roman Empire

typical in Continental Europe and its former colonies

inquisitorial

a court decision is specific to the case before it

favors predictability over flexibility

Constitutions

Court decisions

Statutes

Executive action

Regulations

Primary sources of law

Find one good case.

A legal argument must be supported by **primary sources of law.** If unsure where to begin research, look to **secondary sources**—legal dictionaries and encyclopedias, hornbooks (treatises on an area of the law), practice guides, and law review articles. These will provide an overview of a research topic and will usually reference primary sources, including legal precedents. Once a useful precedent has been identified, almost every case that subsequently cited it can be identified by entering the original case into an online citator service such as Westlaw's KeyCite or Shepard's Citations.

With regards to Bob Berring

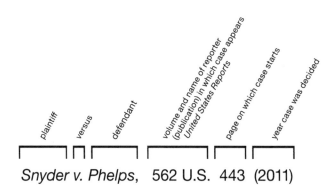

plaintiff versus defendant volume and name of reporter (publication) in which case appears *United States Reports* page on which case starts year case was decided

Snyder v. Phelps, 562 U.S. 443 (2011)

In arguing before a California court, one may cite an unpublished case from Texas, but not an unpublished case from California.

Some, but not all, court decisions are published by the court in **court reporters.** The United States Supreme Court publishes all of its decisions, but some federal courts of appeal publish fewer than 10% of their decisions. Unpublished court decisions generally cannot be used as a basis for argument in the same jurisdiction, as they are not binding precedents. But one may sometimes cite an unpublished decision from another jurisdiction to persuade the court to decide in one's favor.

High court

Intermediate (appeals) court

Trial court

The three-tiered court system

An appeal to an intermediate court is a right. An appeal to a court of last resort is a request.

Trial courts are the primary venues for criminal and civil cases. A litigant dissatisfied with a decision almost always has the right to appeal to an intermediate court.

Intermediate, or appellate, courts typically review a lower court's reasoning and judgment upon appeal by a litigant from a trial court case, and decide whether the trial judge properly interpreted and applied the law. In some instances, the intermediate court may also review the lower court's fact-finding.

High courts consist of a panel of judges who decide which cases they will hear. In some states they are obligated to hear appeals in specific types of cases, such as those involving the death penalty.

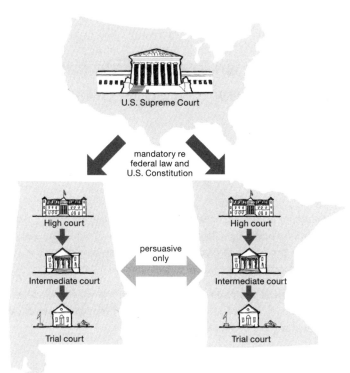

U.S. Supreme Court

mandatory re
federal law and
U.S. Constitution

High court

Intermediate court

Trial court

persuasive
only

High court

Intermediate court

Trial court

An Alabama Supreme Court case is not mandatory authority in a Minnesota court.

A state's highest court is bound by (1) its own previous decisions; and (2) previous decisions of the U.S. Supreme Court in matters involving federal law and the U.S. Constitution.

A state intermediate (appeals) court is bound by (1) its own previous decisions; (2) previous decisions of that state's high court; (3) previous decisions of the U.S. Supreme Court in matters involving federal law and the U.S. Constitution.

A state trial court is bound by (1) its own previous decisions; (2) previous decisions of the intermediate state court for the region the trial court is in; (3) previous decisions of the state's high court; (4) previous decisions of the U.S. Supreme Court in matters involving federal law and the U.S. Constitution.

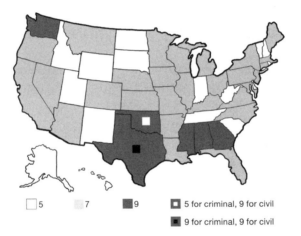

				5 for criminal, 9 for civil
□ 5	▦ 7	■ 9	▣	■ 9 for criminal, 9 for civil

Number of state high court justices

A supreme court might be the lowest court.

Nomenclature in state court systems is not quite universal. Trial courts may be known as circuit courts, superior courts, or courts of common pleas. In California and some other states, the intermediate court is the Court of Appeals. In Maryland it is the Court of Special Appeals, and the highest court is the Court of Appeals. In New York, the highest court is the Court of Appeals, while the lowest court is the Supreme Court.

Texas and Oklahoma each have two courts of last resort—a Supreme Court for civil cases and a Court of Criminal Appeals for criminal cases.

Executive branch

limited power to create law through
proclamations and executive orders

Legislative branch

creates law by
enacting statutes

Judicial branch

creates law through decisions
made in disputes brought to it

Requirement of a controversy

The powers of the three branches of the U.S. government are balanced by a system of checks and balances. The judiciary's power to overrule the other branches is checked by a requirement that it act only on controversies brought to it. In the absence of a court case, it may not initiate new law.

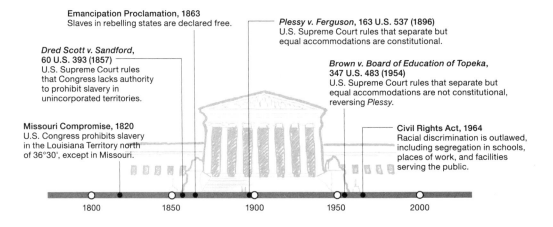

Emancipation Proclamation, 1863
Slaves in rebelling states are declared free.

Plessy v. Ferguson, 163 U.S. 537 (1896)
U.S. Supreme Court rules that separate but equal accommodations are constitutional.

Dred Scott v. Sandford,
60 U.S. 393 (1857)
U.S. Supreme Court rules that Congress lacks authority to prohibit slavery in unincorporated territories.

Brown v. Board of Education of Topeka,
347 U.S. 483 (1954)
U.S. Supreme Court rules that separate but equal accommodations are not constitutional, reversing *Plessy*.

Missouri Compromise, 1820
U.S. Congress prohibits slavery in the Louisiana Territory north of 36°30', except in Missouri.

Civil Rights Act, 1964
Racial discrimination is outlawed, including segregation in schools, places of work, and facilities serving the public.

1800   1850   1900   1950   2000

Sometimes the U.S. Supreme Court overrules the U.S. Supreme Court.

As society advances, discrepancies between the laws established by court precedents and more universal notions of justice may become apparent. This can lead to a court reversing its previous decisions. However, when a court "reverses itself," it doesn't rewrite its earlier decision. Rather, it makes a decision in a new case that contradicts the earlier decision and establishes a new precedent.

"There is no doubt that if there were a super–Supreme Court, a substantial proportion of our reversals of state courts would also be reversed. We are not final because we are infallible, but we are infallible only because we are final."

—ROBERT H. JACKSON, U.S. Supreme Court
Associate Justice, 1941–1954

Attorney Thurgood Marshall, who represented the plaintiffs, became the first African American U.S. Supreme Court Justice in 1967.

Brown v. Board of Education of Topeka, 347 U.S. 483 (1954)

After the Emancipation Proclamation in 1863, policies throughout much of the U.S. supported racial segregation. In *Plessy v. Ferguson*, 163 U.S. 537 (1896), the U.S. Supreme Court ruled that separate facilities for black Americans were acceptable and afforded equal protection under the Fourteenth Amendment.

In 1951, a group of parents of African American schoolchildren filed suit in federal court against the Topeka, Kansas, Board of Education, asserting that segregation provided their children an inferior education. The court ruled against the plaintiffs, holding that black and white schools in Topeka were equal in all regards.

On appeal by the plaintiffs, the U.S. Supreme Court ruled 9–0 that state laws establishing separate schools for black and white students were unconstitutional, thereby reversing its earlier decision in *Plessy*. The court cited several secondary sources in its decision, including:

- Gunnar Myrdal's *An American Dilemma: The Negro Problem and Modern Democracy* (1944)
- Doll test studies by psychologists Kenneth and Mamie Clark, who argued that segregation had a negative emotional impact on black schoolchildren

Small claims

suits between private parties, usually under $10,000

Probate

estates of the deceased

Family

divorce, alimony, child support, custody, adoption

Juvenile

delinquent minors

Traffic

minor motor vehicle violations

Municipal

local ordinances

State courts of limited jurisdiction

Federal courts have limited jurisdiction.

Federal courts may hear only two types of cases:

Diversity cases, i.e., those in which litigants have a diversity of citizenship (such as residents of different states), and potential damages exceed $75,000

Federal question cases, such as those involving international treaties, the U.S. government, the U.S. Constitution, federal statutes, and disputes between states

States also have courts of limited jurisdiction, sometimes referred to as **special courts**. Most cases are heard by a judge rather than a jury. Courts of general jurisdiction sometimes hear appeals from courts of limited jurisdiction.

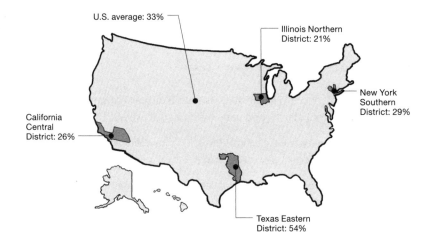

U.S. average: 33%

Illinois Northern
District: 21%

New York
Southern
District: 29%

California
Central
District: 26%

Texas Eastern
District: 54%

Patentee victory rates in federal patent infringement claims, 1997–2016
Source: 2017 Patent Litigation Study, PWC

Erie Railroad Co. v. Tompkins, 304 U.S. 64 (1938)

Harry Tompkins was walking at night on an Erie Railroad right-of-way in Pennsylvania. A protrusion from a passing train knocked him down, and a train wheel crushed his arm. Pennsylvania law required that Tompkins, a trespasser, show that Erie had acted with "wanton negligence" in order to hold it liable. But Tompkins sued in federal court in New York, where Erie was incorporated, and where he had to show that Erie had acted with mere "ordinary negligence." Tompkins successfully argued for applying the federal standard.

Erie's appeals eventually reached the U.S. Supreme Court, which ruled that courts must apply the law of the state in which an incident occurs. The decision greatly limited **forum shopping,** the practice of suing in the court most likely to favor one's claims. Litigants in some types of cases, however, such as patent infringements, continued to have access to multiple federal courts. But in 2017, the Supreme Court ruled that patent suits must be filed in the jurisdiction in which an accused infringer is incorporated, or in which it committed the alleged infringement and has a regular place of business. But Americans continue to forum shop when possible—for example by filing defamation suits in the United Kingdom, where laws tend to favor plaintiffs.

Patent

Copyright

**101 Things
I Learned**®

Trademark

Trade secret

Intellectual property rights

A copyright doesn't protect an idea.

Only the tangible expression of an idea, not an idea itself, can be protected by a copyright. If a screenplay is copyrighted, others may not copy or use it or significant portions without permission. But a copyright doesn't prevent others from writing their own screenplay using the same ideas. It may seem unfair that the law allows someone to use another's valued ideas, but this is in the best interest of society, as it encourages citizens to act on, rather than sit on, new ideas.

The law creates fictional characters.

21

The eggshell (thin skull) plaintiff: A defendant can be liable for a plaintiff's unforeseeable and uncommon reactions. For example, one who negligently scrapes a hemophiliac may be liable for all the plaintiff's injuries, even though the same harm to another person would have been minor.

The fertile octogenarian: Under the law of estates and trusts, a woman is presumed capable of giving birth until she dies.

The corporation: An abstract entity that, like a person, may own property, enter into contracts, sue and be sued, be held liable under civil and criminal law, and even have some constitutional rights.

The reasonable person: An imaginary individual placed in the circumstances of a litigant or other party at the time of a given action. For example, in a negligence case a reasonable person acts sensibly and without undue delay.

Institutions

Trustees of estates

Corporations

Infants (via guardian)

Municipalities

Individuals

Parties that often have standing

You have to stand to sue.

A plaintiff has **standing** if it is the proper party to request that the court hear and rule on a legal controversy. Three overlapping requirements generally must be met:

1 **The plaintiff must have suffered or is imminently likely to suffer an injury.**

2 **The named defendant must be the cause of the plaintiff's injury.** A plaintiff lacks standing if the injury cannot be traced to the defendant's behavior, or if it is the result of an act by a third party not named in the suit.

3 **The injury must be redressable through the court.** A favorable ruling from the court must be likely to compensate for, or fix the wrong cited by, the plaintiff.

"A ship has a legal personality, a fiction found useful for maritime purposes. . . . So it should be as respects valleys, alpine meadows, rivers, lakes, estuaries, beaches, ridges, groves of trees, swampland, or even air that feels the destructive pressures of modern technology and modern life. . . . The voice of the inanimate object, therefore, should not be stilled."

23

—WILLIAM O. DOUGLAS, U.S. Supreme Court Associate Justice, dissenting opinion in *Sierra Club v. Morton*, 405 U.S. 727 (1972)

Denzel Washington as attorney Joe Miller in *Philadelphia* (1993)

Explain it to an eight-year-old.

The "bones" of a case—its essential facts and structure, and the argument you are making in support of your position—should be understandable in simple terms. If you can explain it to a child, you can explain it to a jury.

A lawyer is an incrementalist.

Even the most inventive, aggressive, and original legal argument is constructed upon that which came before—prior court cases, constitutions, and existing statutes and regulations. This may seem limiting, but ultimately it is freeing, for the legal arena presents an opportunity found in few professional settings: to walk others down your argument path one step at a time, without interruption, from an established starting point.

The theory of a case

The theory of a case is the single most plausible storyline of a litigating position. It is the core around which all points of a case are organized and presented, the idea that remains standing should all else be taken away. It is both a logical and emotional center: it is consistent with every piece of evidence the judge or jury will accept, and it considers the subjective positions taken by the litigants and likely to be taken by the judge and jury. There should be only one theory, consisting of a few sentences, that will always tell you where you are and where you need to go when in the midst of an oral argument, deposition, or research.

- "My client killed her estranged husband because she had been an abused spouse and she knew he had come to her home to kill her. She acted in self-defense."
- "The defendant deliberately concealed information from my client, knowing that my client would not have signed the contract had she been aware of it."
- "The crowd was throwing snowballs when the defendant fired his gun, killing two men. Snowballs, not rocks. The defendant overreacted, and must be held accountable."

Insight doesn't arrive head-on.

Be suspicious of the person who sizes up a new situation very quickly, claims understanding, and stakes out an ironclad position. Insight usually requires long periods of discussion, research, analysis, rationalization, and counterargument, and it rarely arrives while attacking a matter directly or on a first pass. If one occasionally is able to quickly understand a complex matter, he or she is far more likely to quickly *mis*understand it.

"I made three arguments in every case. First came the one I had planned—as I thought, logical, coherent, complete. Second was the one actually presented—interrupted, incoherent, disjointed, disappointing. The third was the utterly devastating argument that I thought of after going to bed that night."

28

—ROBERT H. JACKSON, "Advocacy Before the Supreme Court: Suggestions for Effective Case Presentations" (1951)

Give your witnesses a home base.

It can be difficult for a witness to remain calm and composed if the opposing attorney asks questions for which the witness has not prepared, uses unexpected wording, or asks a series of questions that leads the witness toward a position he or she does not believe to be true.

When preparing witnesses for trial, identify a home base from which testimony is to emerge. A home base is not a rehearsed answer but a core position inherent in a witness's relationship to and knowledge of the case. Although it may be different for each witness, each home base grows out of and directly supports the case's central theory.

Leading questions

Non-leading questions

A hostile witness can be helpful.

Friendly witnesses are those called to give testimony in support of one's own case. **Hostile witnesses** are called by the opposing party. An examining attorney may ask **leading questions**—those calling for yes/no responses—only of the opposing party's witnesses. However, if a friendly witness is evasive or uncooperative, the examining attorney may request permission from the judge to treat the witness as hostile. If granted, the attorney may ask leading questions, allowing the attorney much tighter control of the examination.

Avoid asking a question in court if you don't already know the answer.

A trial is not the time and place to be surprised by the answer to a question. It's better to be surprised during pre-trial discovery.

When an answer to a question would be quite obvious and favorable to your case, it is sometimes effective to not ask it at all, and to leave the general awareness of it hanging in the courtroom air.

Ways to discredit a witness

32

Bias: Show that the witness is testifying under an immunity agreement or plea bargain, has a personal relationship with someone involved in the case, or is being paid for expertise.

Contradiction: Show that a witness's testimony is inconsistent with that of other witnesses or evidence, is contradicted by previous statements by the witness (e.g., deposition), or is selective or incomplete.

Character: Show that the witness has been dishonest in other statements or actions, or has criminal convictions suggesting dishonesty.

Limitations: Show that the witness's view was obstructed, or that the witness has abnormal memory due to mental incapacity or intoxication.

Expertise: Show that credentials are inadequate or not specific to the subject, or that the purity of the evidence evaluated by the expert is in question.

33

Witnesses were once "suits."

Before the development of a coherent legal system in England in the 12th century, a plaintiff substantiated a claim by bringing to local decision makers a **suit**—a group of witnesses who supported his position against a defendant. Thus the plaintiff literally "brought a suit" to the trier of fact.

Trial

a formal, evidence-based
procedure conducted in court
to determine a verdict

Hearing

a comparatively informal
administrative procedure to
determine a limited matter

Put some length in your briefs, but keep your motions short.

A **motion** is a written or oral request to the court, made before, during, or even after a legal proceeding, to rule on a specific issue, such as to disallow certain testimony, dismiss charges, or request a new trial. Motions should be kept short and simple so that the court may understand what is being asked of it. The place to elaborate on a motion is in a **brief**—a persuasive written document filed with the court, setting forth one's legal and factual arguments. A brief is a lawyer's only means, other than oral presentation, of arguing to the judge.

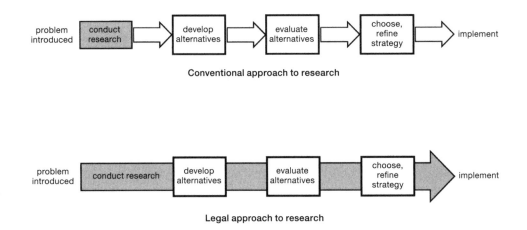

problem introduced → conduct research → develop alternatives → evaluate alternatives → choose, refine strategy → implement

Conventional approach to research

problem introduced → conduct research → develop alternatives → evaluate alternatives → choose, refine strategy → implement

Legal approach to research

Research isn't finished until the deadline arrives.

35

Research is a primary, not preliminary, activity. Through research, one finds the law that supports an argument, that may argue against it, and that may mitigate any counterarguments. New precedents emerge constantly, up to and concurrently with the presentation of a closing argument.

With regards to Bob Berring

Issues

identify matter(s) of
concern in the
current case

Rule of law

from prior cases:
identify and explain how
it was interpreted

Application

compare facts to your
issue and apply rule of
law to current case

Conclusion

a summary that
follows naturally from
the preceding

The IRAC sequence of argument

Writing isn't recording your thoughts; it's thinking on the page.

A well-constructed argument rarely, if ever, resembles what one started with. Writing effectively isn't recording the argument one wishes to make; it is a process of discovering what one's argument needs to be. Through writing, thinking, researching, rewriting, rethinking, and rewriting again, an argument is discovered and clarified.

"Every judgment I write tells a lie against itself. . . . The actual journey of a judgment starts with the most tentative exploratory ideas, and passes through large swathes of doubt and contestation before finally ending up as a confident exposition purportedly excluding any possibility of error. The erratic, even contradictory pathways, are hidden."

37

—ALBIE SACHS, former justice,
Constitutional Court of South Africa

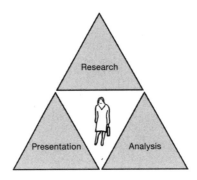

Skills for a lawyer

Good argument trumps good facts . . . if you're a student.

Lawyers ideally have good facts, good law, and good arguments. Students benefit from all three, but above all must develop and demonstrate the ability to make good arguments. Whether working from good or bad facts, or good or bad law, students need to show they can use their resources to convincingly support or refute a position.

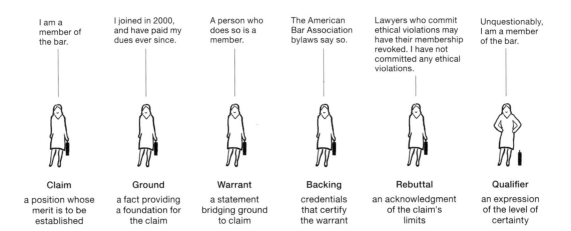

I am a
member of
the bar.

I joined in 2000,
and have paid my
dues ever since.

A person who
does so is a
member.

The American
Bar Association
bylaws say so.

Lawyers who commit
ethical violations may
have their membership
revoked. I have not
committed any ethical
violations.

Unquestionably,
I am a member
of the bar.

Claim
a position whose
merit is to be
established

Ground
a fact providing
a foundation for
the claim

Warrant
a statement
bridging ground
to claim

Backing
credentials
that certify
the warrant

Rebuttal
an acknowledgment
of the claim's
limits

Qualifier
an expression
of the level of
certainty

The Toulmin Model of Argument
Adapted from Toulmin, Stephen. *The Uses of Argument.*
Updated ed. Cambridge, England: Cambridge University Press, 2003.

Don't try to prove you are objectively right; show that your position is preferable to the alternative.

39

It is always possible to make at least some arguments for or against a legal position. An argument requires logic, but legal argument is not a purely logical form of argument that promises a universal, absolute conclusion. Rather, it is a practical form of argument that aims to establish one claim as more probable or reasonable than another.

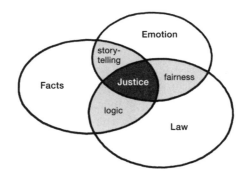

If the law is in your favor, pound the law. If the facts are in your favor, pound the facts. If neither is in your favor, pound the table.

Few judges will rule against clear precedent. When the law favors your position, identify it and return to it again and again. If the law does not clearly favor your argument, emphasize the facts of the case most likely to engender sympathy for your client, so the judge or jury might favorably interpret any gray areas in the law.

And on second thought: don't pound the table.

Be the most reasonable person in the room.

Lawyers are officers of the court, as are judges, bailiffs, and other court personnel. All are obligated to safeguard the proper comportment of the judicial process. Projecting that one is careful, knowledgeable, thoughtful, and considerate is more important than projecting that one is to be feared. Even if others act poorly, you cannot use it as a reason to act poorly yourself.

Caucasians are pink.
Spam is pink.
Bubblegum is pink.
My dog's tongue is pink.
There must be other pink things.

Caucasians are pink.
I am Caucasian.
I am pink.

I am pink.
Spam is pink.
I'm pink; therefore I'm Spam.

Proper induction

premises suggest
likely conclusion

Proper deduction

premises guarantee
truth of conclusion

Improper deduction

premises do not
suggest conclusion

Make a logical argument.

Deductive logic usually works from broadly accepted truths toward a demonstration of truth in a specific situation. More generally, it is any logical line of reasoning in which the premises guarantee a true outcome.

Inductive logic tends to work from specific truths toward a demonstration of a larger, more encompassing truth. However, it can be any line of reasoning in which the conclusion, although not guaranteed, is a likely or highly probable outcome of the premises. Good inductive reasoning requires a convincingly large sample size.

The defendant
mercilessly
killed his boss.

Weak

The defendant aimed a rusty musket
at his boss's face and callously pulled
the trigger. The bullet entered his
skull through his right eye socket.
He died over the course of three
hours. His children, ages one, two,
and seven, never saw him again.

Stronger

Tell a compelling story.

A proper argument is not driven by emotion, but if an argument lacks an emotional component, it is unlikely to connect with a judge or jury. Convey facts accurately, but also set a scene so the audience can connect to events and characters. Emotions attach to details, not to abstractions and generalities.

With regards to Bill Fernholz

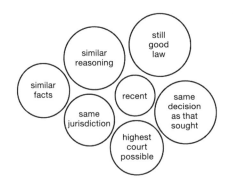

Components of a good precedent

Let your citations argue for you.

In legal writing, almost every sentence, whether discussing law or fact, should be followed by a reference to a source. Otherwise, the decision maker is left to assume a statement is merely what the attorney believes, but cannot prove, is true.

Master the transitions.

Addition: Also, And, Another reason, Besides, Equally important, Finally, Furthermore, In addition, In other words, Moreover, Next, Similarly

Alternative: Alternatively, Although, But, Contrary to, Conversely, Even though, However, In contrast, Nevertheless, On the other hand, Regardless, Still, Though, Yet

Analogy: Again, Also, Analogously, Likewise, Similarly

45

Concluding: Accordingly, All in all, As a result, Consequently, Finally, Hence, In short, In summary, Lastly, Therefore, Thus, To summarize

Establishing a causal consequence: As a result, Because, Consequently, It follows, Since, Then, Therefore, Thus

Introducing an example: For example, For instance, In particular, Namely, Specifically, That is

Signaling a concession: Although, Granted, It is true, No doubt, To be sure

Signaling that one is about to speak about a client's case: Here, In the case at hand, In the present matter

The defendant shot the victim and hid the gun in his garage.

Active voice

indicates direct connection

Yes, a gun was found in the defendant's garage. However, other events account for this.

Passive voice

suggests incidental relationship

Sometimes passive voice is stronger.

Statements made in the active voice indicate direct connections and are usually more effective for argument. Passive voice suggests incidental connections, and tends to sound weaker and less convincing. However, there are occasions when passive voice is the more effective form—particularly when one's precise point is that a connection is merely coincidental.

46

Something reasonable is reasonable, not "not unreasonable."

It's fine to *count* things; you don't have to *enumerate* them. If something happened *at that point in time*, it happened *then*. If an event occurred *as a result of the fact of x*, it occurred *because of x*. If the *alleged perpetrator was observed carrying an unidentified implement on his person in the course of events ensuing subsequent to a crime*, the *defendant carried something after a crime*.

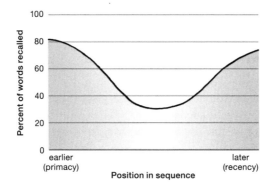

The Recency Effect

Stop talking when you've made your point.

Begin and end every argument or talking point with the thing you most want the listener to note or remember. Early points tend to be remembered by listeners because they aren't competing with all the other points to come. As one continues to speak, each new word or idea must compete for space in the listener's memory.

Items at the end of a talk tend to be better remembered because they are recent in memory, and are perhaps still in the "working" portion of one's memory. Additionally, listener interest is elevated at the conclusion because it is understood as the summing-up of previous points made—and perhaps not listened to.

48

How to misunderstand a contract

Unilateral mistake: One party is in error as to a contract's terms or subject matter. The contract will usually be upheld by the court. However, courts may void or revise a contract if the non-mistaken party was aware of and tried to take advantage of the mistake, or if enforcement would be unconscionable (e.g., a very one-sided contract).

Mutual mistake: Both parties are mistaken as to the meaning of a contract term. The mistakes may be different from each other (e.g., two interpretations of a word), or they may be the same, such as a shared misunderstanding of an external fact (e.g., "to occur on February 29, 2023"). Some courts call the former a mutual mistake and the latter a **common mistake**. Courts usually will revise the contract if possible, or nullify it if the mistake makes performance impossible.

49

The *Peerless* Case

Two businessmen, Raffles and Wichelhaus, entered into a contract for the sale of 125 bales of cotton. Shipment from India to England was to be made on the British ship *Peerless*. Unknown to both parties, there were two ships of this name. Wichelhaus, the receiver, expected shipment on the *Peerless* arriving in October. Unfortunately, it was carried on the other *Peerless*, which arrived in December. Wichelhaus refused to accept the delivery.

Raffles sued Wichelhaus for breach of contract, but the court was unable to determine which ship named *Peerless* was intended in the written agreement. As it could not be shown that the parties had agreed to the same thing, there was no **meeting of the minds** and therefore no binding contract. The court ruled that Wichelhaus did not have to pay for the cotton.

Although from British law, the *Peerless* case (*Raffles v. Wichelhaus* [1864] EWHC Exch J19) is well known in American law because it helped establish the concept of the meeting of the minds—and likely because of the irony of there being two ships named *Peerless*.

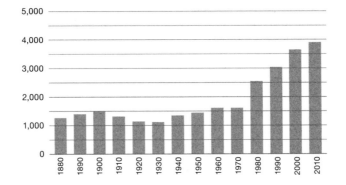

50

Number of lawyers in U.S. per 100,000 citizens
Sources: American Bar Association and U.S. Census Bureau

A lawyer may not practice law with a non-lawyer, unless the non-lawyer is in jail.

Anyone may give legal advice, but the recipient has to know if it is from a lawyer. For this reason, a lawyer may not enter into a business enterprise with a non-lawyer if its activities include the practice of law. A client could become confused as to the source and reliability of advice, and whether communications with the firm are privileged. However, a lawyer is permitted to assist the legal efforts of a "jailhouse lawyer"—a prisoner who provides legal advice to other prisoners.

51

Damages

payment for
plaintiff's losses

Specific performance or injunction

litigant must perform or cease
performing a specific act

Declaratory remedy

rights and obligations
of litigants clarified

Some civil remedies

One cannot simply sue, but must sue for *something*.

A plaintiff must request a specific **remedy,** such as a payment it wishes the defendant to make or an action it wants the defendant to take or stop taking. A plaintiff cannot ask the court to issue an advisory opinion, make a public statement on an issue, or edit a statute.

52

If waiting for a final decision from the court might prove ineffectual to a plaintiff, he or she may request an **injunction**—a court order that the opposing party do or stop doing an act—at any time.

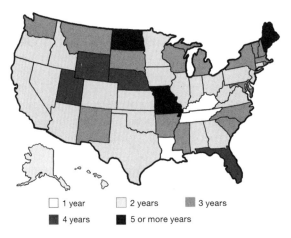

Statutes of limitations on personal injury claims
Source: Nolo

You can't sleep on your rights.

The law limits how long after an injury has occurred, or has been discovered to have occurred, that a claim or charge can be brought. A **statute of limitations** serves to provide a sense of finality and predictability for the defendant, and to make sure a claim can be resolved while evidence is available, memories are fresh, and testimony may be considered reliable.

Try not to harm—even while being helpful.

Good Samaritan laws exist to excuse harms caused by a person who voluntarily renders assistance to someone in distress. They help counter the reluctance people may feel to help an imperiled stranger. However, Good Samaritan laws can vary widely, and even a well-intentioned helper may be successfully sued for negligence in some jurisdictions.

Actual damages

an award for direct
injury or loss

**Consequential
damages**

an award for
indirect costs

Future damages

for expected losses, e.g.,
medical expenses,
reduced income

Punitive damages

punishes defendant for
recklessness, malice, or deceit

**Attorney's
fees**

Common civil awards

An injured party has a responsibility to minimize the damage.

In many jurisdictions, a party suffering a personal injury cannot recover for losses incurred by failing to seek reasonable medical care, unless the conduct that caused the injury was willful or done in bad faith.

55

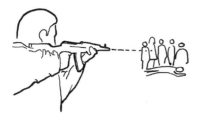

Foreseeable

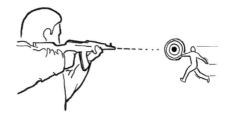

Not foreseeable

Palsgraf v. Long Island Railroad Co., 248 N.Y. 339 (1928)

A man carrying an ordinary-looking package was hurrying to board a moving train. A railroad employee helped pull the passenger into the rail car while another employee pushed. The package was dislodged and fell. Unfortunately, it contained fireworks and exploded. The force knocked down a scale at the other end of the platform, injuring a Mrs. Palsgraf.

Palsgraf sued the railroad, claiming her injury resulted from negligent acts by its employees. She won, but on appeal the highest court in New York dismissed Palsgraf's complaint, holding that it was not **foreseeable** that her injuries would result from the employees' actions. The court's decision means a defendant, even one who acts negligently, is not automatically liable for all consequences of his or her actions.

56

Pleading

the plaintiff files a complaint;
the defendant answers, demurs,
or files a cross-complaint

Discovery and motion practice

evidence and sworn
statements are exchanged;
pre-trial motions are filed

Trial

facts and arguments are
presented before a judge or
judge and jury

The three stages of a civil case

Most of what happens in a civil trial happened before the trial.

In civil cases, litigants exchange information before trial. Through the **discovery process,** each party may depose (question under oath) the opposition and any other individuals who may provide relevant information. Each side typically knows the other side's case before the trial begins.

A judge is also involved before trial. A judge reads pre-trial pleadings and motions from the two sides, researches relevant legal issues, settles disputes that arise during discovery, issues warrants and summonses, and supervises jury selection. Most cases settle before trial, making pre-trial work the main work for lawyers as well as the court.

57

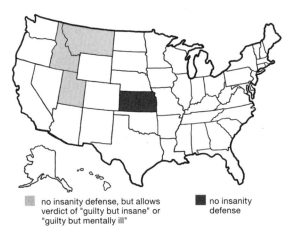

no insanity defense, but allows verdict of "guilty but insane" or "guilty but mentally ill"

no insanity defense

States not allowing an insanity defense

The party that alleges bears the burden of proof.

Each party in a dispute bears the burden of proving its allegations. A party that denies an allegation has no obligation to disprove it, with few exceptions. A criminal defendant who enters a plea of **not guilty by reason of insanity,** for example, takes on a burden of proving insanity.

In a few types of civil disputes, the defendant bears the burden of proof. For example, a customer sued by a utility provider for nonpayment may have to prove that the bill was paid, or provide a convincing justification for why it was not.

58

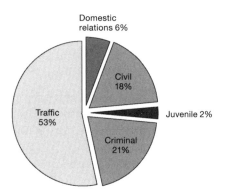

Domestic
relations 6%

Civil
18%

Juvenile 2%

Traffic
53%

Criminal
21%

Incoming cases, all U.S. state courts, 2016
Source: Court Statistics Project

The party that alleges gets to argue twice.

Opening statements: The plaintiff or prosecutor presents an initial summary of its case. The opposing party follows.

Plaintiff/prosecutor's case-in-chief: The plaintiff/prosecutor calls its witnesses for direct examination. After each, the defense may conduct a cross-examination. The plaintiff/prosecutor may then re-question each witness regarding matters that emerged from cross-examination.

Defendant's case-in-chief: The defense calls its witnesses for direct examination. After each, the plaintiff/prosecutor may cross-examine. The defense may re-question each witness on matters that emerged from cross-examination.

Rebuttal case: The plaintiff/prosecutor may request to proceed with rebuttal evidence in response to the defendant's case-in-chief. The judge may allow the defendant to rebut the plaintiff/prosecutor's rebuttal, if it introduced new matters.

When either side completes its case-in-chief, defense, or rebuttal, it indicates that it rests. Counsel may reopen a closed phase of the trial only with permission.

Closing arguments: Plaintiff/prosecutor; defendant; then plaintiff/prosecutor.

Deliberations and verdict.

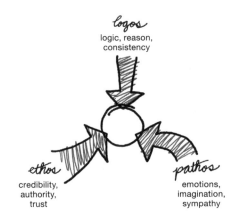

logos
logic, reason,
consistency

ethos
credibility,
authority,
trust

pathos
emotions,
imagination,
sympathy

Keep it slightly above room temperature.

Rationality is cool; passion is warm. Rationality provides logical justification for a position, while passion provides a human connection to it. Both are needed to advance an argument; an abundance of one will not compensate for a dearth of the other. An argument may be extraordinarily rational, but its correctness alone is unlikely to compel others to care enough to right the alleged wrongs. An extremely passionate argument may initially attract sympathy, but unmitigated displays of emotion at the expense of rationality will wear thin and eventually prompt others to tune out your message.

Rationality makes an argument worthy. Passion makes it worthwhile.

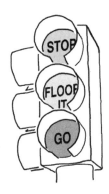

What's in dispute—facts or law?

Law: A statute requires a paroled sex offender to live at least 2,000 feet from a school.
Facts: The parolee already owns a home less than 2,000 feet from a school, and nearly all other residences in the community are similarly sited.
Question for the court: Is a law constitutional if it promotes a parolee's homelessness?

Law: The vehicle code requires motorists to stop at red lights.
Facts: A police officer cites a motorist for running a red light. The defendant says the light was red, but that he went through it to make way for a fire truck.
Question for the court: Was the defendant making way for an emergency vehicle, and does this mean he should be excused for breaking the law?

Law: Contracts require both parties to have the same understanding of their critical terms.
Facts: Party A agreed to purchase arms from Party B. Party B delivered a shipment of mannequin limbs to the buyer, who was expecting munitions.
Question for the court: Did one party or the other conceal its awareness of the other's misunderstanding at the time of contract?

Laws regulating
individual conduct

Laws providing for
state services

Laws empowering
or directing local
governments

Laws determining
raising and
spending of money

Amendments
to the state
constitution

Five categories of statutes in the State of North Carolina

When meaning is contested, look to intent.

When the meaning of a statute is disputed, courts look to legislative intent (the policy and broader legislative scheme behind it); language (composition, structure, qualifying words, technical versus general meaning); and history (events leading to and following the legislation).

When the meaning of a contract term is disputed, courts generally look to what the parties intended when they entered into the contract. If a specific word is in dispute, courts usually presume the generally accepted meaning unless one party can prove that a narrower or more specialized meaning is its proper interpretation.

62

Zealous advocacy

for client, within
legal bounds

Loyalty

cannot assume a position
adverse to client's interest

Confidentiality

must maintain confidences of
clients and potential clients

Limited solicitation

of prospective
clients

Competence

must have appropriate skills,
time, and qualifications

Communication

must keep client
well informed

Ethics for lawyers

A marijuana-related business may not declare bankruptcy.

Cannabis cultivation and sale are permitted by some states but are prohibited by federal law, while bankruptcy proceedings are governed by federal law. The intersection of these laws means that the federal bankruptcy courts will not allow a cannabis-related business to use its process. Similarly, the U.S. Patent and Trademark Office will not issue a trademark registration to a cannabis-related business.

Discrepancies between federal and state laws can present ethical dilemmas for a lawyer. State ethics rules for lawyers typically prohibit advising a client to violate the laws of the United States. But by advising a cannabis producer how to legally run his farm under state law, a lawyer may be advising the farmer to engage in criminal activity under federal law.

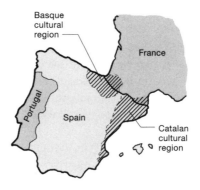

Non-aligning political and cultural boundaries

Four types of boundaries

Political boundaries define sovereign or locally sovereign entities such as cities, counties, states, and nations. They are the product of numerous, often competing factors, including geography, culture, long-term settlement patterns, conquest, and negotiation.

Electoral boundaries establish voting areas for legislative bodies. They partly or mostly coincide with political boundaries, but must be altered with some frequency to accommodate shifts in population distribution. Gerrymandering is the manipulation of electoral boundaries by a political party to create electoral districts whose demographics favor its candidates.

64

Jurisdictional boundaries define the regions by which court systems are organized. They typically align with political boundaries, although they may cross them, as in the case of U.S. federal circuit courts.

Cultural boundaries demarcate a region whose inhabitants' language, social customs, and other practices differ from those of surrounding areas. Cultural boundaries often cross other types of boundaries.

Navajo Nation

There are more than 300 nations within the United States.

The U.S. Constitution grants **local sovereignty** to over 300 American Indian reservations. They cannot enter into treaties with foreign entities, but Indian nations have their own court systems to adjudicate matters involving Indian affairs on tribal land. They cannot adjudicate matters involving non-Indians.

The total land area of all Indian reservations in the U.S. is 87,800 square miles, approximately the size of Minnesota. Navajo Nation, at over 27,000 square miles, is larger than 10 U.S. states, and 12 reservations are each larger than Rhode Island, the smallest U.S. state.

65

Jails

run by sheriffs or local governments;
house inmates awaiting trial or convicts serving short sentences

Prisons

run by state or federal governments;
detain individuals serving longer
sentences for serious crimes

Felonies, misdemeanors, and wobblers

Felony: a serious crime, usually punishable by imprisonment for more than one year. Includes arson, assault, battery, burglary, grand larceny, grand theft, multiple-offense DUI, murder, rape, robbery, serious drug offenses, unauthorized possession of a deadly weapon, and vandalism of federal property.

Misdemeanor: a crime less serious than a felony, usually punishable by a fine, forfeiture, or less than a year in prison or jail. Includes disorderly conduct, first-offense DUI, petty theft, possession of small amounts of some drugs, prostitution, public intoxication, reckless driving, simple assault, trespassing, and vandalism.

66

Wobbler: a crime that can be charged as a felony or misdemeanor, depending on circumstance; for example, if there is an aggravating factor. Some felonies may be reduced to misdemeanors during sentencing or even after conviction.

	State crimes	**Federal crimes**
Pre-trial discovery	Occurs early in proceedings, long before trial	Prosecutor not required to provide witness statements until after witness testifies
Sentencing	Mandatory minimums for some crimes, but a judge may be lenient in unusual circumstances	Severe mandatory minimums based on the offense and defendant's criminal history

If you're going to spray graffiti, don't do it on the post office.

Typically prosecuted in state court	Typically prosecuted in federal court
Assault & battery	Bank robbery/bank fraud
Domestic violence	Bribery of public officials; public corruption
Embezzlement	Child pornography
Fraud	Crimes committed on federal property
Most misdemeanors	Crimes involving state-to-state flight
Murder	Export crimes
Operating under the influence	Mail and wire fraud/theft
Possession of controlled substances	Money laundering
Rape/sex crimes/child molestation	Securities fraud
Robbery/theft	Tax crimes
Trafficking in controlled substances not crossing state lines	Trafficking in controlled substances across state or federal lines

67

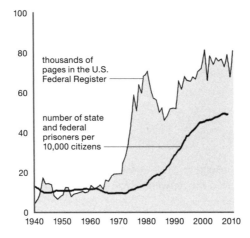

thousands of pages in the U.S. Federal Register

number of state and federal prisoners per 10,000 citizens

Sources: U.S. Department of Justice, U.S. Census Bureau, and Office of the Federal Register

"The more laws and order are made prominent, the more thieves and robbers there will be."

—LAO-TZU

68

Just don't inhale.

You're allowed to puff.

If you're selling something and you fudge a little, it's OK. You're allowed to exaggerate how good something is in an effort to make a sale, as long as you are expressing an opinion and not misrepresenting a fact. Some **puffing** is expected of any salesperson.

	Involuntary manslaughter	Voluntary manslaughter	Second-degree murder	First-degree murder
Did killer intend to kill?	No	Sometimes	Usually	Yes
Did killing result from negligence?	Yes	No	No	No
Was killing premeditated?	No	No	No	Yes
Was killing result of "heat of passion"?	N.A.	Sometimes	Sometimes	N.A.

Common homicide standards

Intent can be essential; motive rarely is.

Motive is the reason one has for committing a crime. It can help the prosecution identify and indict a defendant, but it doesn't provide direct evidence of guilt. Personal financial difficulty, for example, could suggest an individual had a motive to commit a robbery, but it provides no better than circumstantial evidence.

Intent is the resolution to commit a crime. A defendant's possession of tools for breaking a safe suggests an intent to commit burglary and theft, and may serve as direct evidence of guilt.

Motive is not essential to the court when guilt is clearly established by the evidence. But if the prosecution's case is based largely on circumstantial evidence, motive might be a persuasive consideration—for either guilt or innocence.

 + =

Guilty act + guilty mind = Guilty

Actus non facit reum nisi mens sit rea means "An act does not make one guilty unless his mind is also guilty." For a defendant to be found guilty of most crimes, he must have some awareness that his act was criminal.

When a defendant enters a plea of **not guilty by reason of insanity,** he is arguing he lacked *mens rea*—the capacity to appreciate why his actions were wrong. In some states, an insanity plea allows an "irresistible impulse" defense, which says the defendant understood his behavior was wrong but was unable to control it.

In civil cases, a defendant can be held liable without demonstration of *mens rea*. But if it is successfully demonstrated, the award for damages is often increased.

71

General deterrence

discouraging criminal acts
through public displays
of punishment

Specific deterrence

reducing offenders' ability to
commit future crimes through
incarceration/incapacitation

Rehabilitation

reducing future crimes
by helping offenders
become productive

Retribution

discouraging crime by
issuing punishment in
proportion to severity

Watchful eye

reducing crime through
fear or embarrassment
of being caught

Broken window theory

discouraging aggressive
crime patterns by repairing
evidence of small infractions

Crime deterrence

A criminal defendant may have to conduct a criminal investigation.

Civil litigants are entitled to acquire sworn pre-trial depositions from the opposing side through the discovery process. But a criminal defendant usually does not have the right to interview the prosecution or its witnesses. Consequently, a trial is often a criminal defense attorney's first opportunity to question the prosecution's witnesses.

The prosecution is required, however, to provide to the defense a list of its witnesses as well as any potentially exculpatory evidence it possesses. To avoid being surprised at trial, a criminal defendant and/or his attorney often have to hire a private investigator to identify additional evidence to support their case.

Hourly fee

usually billed in
1/10 hr. increments

Contingency fee

percentage of
award to client

Flat fee

payable regardless
of outcome

Contingency fees are prohibited in criminal cases.

A contingency fee is payable to an attorney only upon the successful outcome of a civil case. In a criminal case, a contingency fee could create a conflict of interest—for example, in a murder case in which the defendant is the named beneficiary of the victim's life insurance policy. If the defense attorney's fee was based on the policy payout, she would not get paid if the defendant pleaded guilty via a plea bargain, and thereby would have no incentive to plea bargain on behalf of the client—even if it was in the client's best interest.

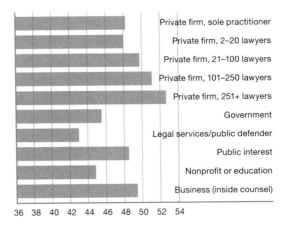

Answer to, "How many hours did you work last week?"
Source: "After the JD III," American Bar Foundation, 2016

An hour might be 116 minutes long.

Lawyers usually bill in 6-minute (1/10 hour) increments. A 3.1-minute phone con-versation could result in a bill for 6 minutes.

74

Invoking the Fifth Amendment in a criminal trial prevents self-incrimination. Invoking it in a civil trial may *induce* self-incrimination.

The Fifth Amendment to the U.S. Constitution grants citizens accused of a crime the right to remain silent to avoid incriminating themselves. Witnesses in a civil trial may invoke this right only if a statement might implicate them in a crime for which later prosecution is possible. The court is usually entitled to make an **adverse inference** against a civil witness who does so.

75

Spousal

Academic research

Reporter

Psychotherapeutic

Clergy-communicant

Congressional

Informer

Executive

Common privileges

If a client brings a friend to a meeting with an attorney, privilege may be lost.

Attorney-client privilege forbids a lawyer from disclosing certain communications made with a client—when those communications were intended by the client to be confidential—to anyone else without the client's permission. However, if the client brings a third party to a meeting with his or her attorney, and the third party is not there to further the client's interests, it may be implied that the client did not intend for communications made in the meeting to be confidential.

76

Watkins told me he was bangin' with the Van Buren Boys.

Hearsay

If intended to prove Watkins was a gang member

Watkins told me he was bangin' with the Van Buren Boys.

Not hearsay

If intended only to show an expert's expertise

You don't know the rule until you know the exceptions.

A presumption of all court testimony is that the opposing side may cross-examine its source. If a witness attributes a statement to someone who is not available to be cross-examined, the statement, if objected to by the opposing attorney, might be ruled **hearsay** and be forbidden.

The rule against hearsay testimony has about thirty exceptions. To get a statement made outside court into court when its originator is unavailable to testify, one has to determine how to fit it into at least one of the exceptions. In practice, the exceptions to the rule *are* the rule.

Hire a lawyer, even if you are one.

Expertise: Lawyers are specialists. Being a good lawyer in one area of the law is rarely a satisfactory substitute for hiring a specialist who intimately knows the relevant law, unique terminology, and best expert witnesses for a particular type of case.

Objectivity: Developing an effective litigation strategy calls for viewing a case from the outside, without anger, desire for revenge, or other emotional distortions.

Showmanship: Hiring a lawyer tells the other side you are serious about your complaint, or about defending yourself against a complaint, giving you a stronger position in any settlement negotiations.

Circumstantial evidence may be more damning than direct evidence.

Direct evidence supports an assertion without need for other evidence or inferences. Eyewitness testimony is a common form of direct evidence, as it directly supports the prosecution's case against a defendant.

Circumstantial evidence has more than one possible interpretation, and must be connected to other evidence or inferences to indicate a defendant's direct connection to a crime. If multiple sources provide such testimony, such that each checks and reinforces the others, a convincing argument may be made. By contrast, a single instance of direct eyewitness testimony may be faulty or driven by ulterior motives.

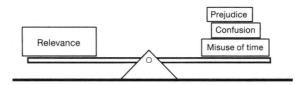

Useful evidence may not be admissible evidence.

Relevance: Is the evidence connected to the issues at trial? Will it make an important alleged fact in the case more or less probable?

Authentication: Can the evidence be shown to be what its proponent says it is? Can a proper chain of custody be demonstrated—for example, by bringing to court the police officer who found the evidence?

Hearsay: If the source of the evidence cannot appear in court, can the evidence be admitted under a hearsay exception?

Privileges: Will any privileges (spousal, attorney-client, etc.) prevent the evidence from being admitted?

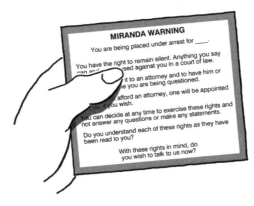

Miranda v. Arizona, 384 U.S. 436 (1966)

A few days before his twenty-second birthday in 1963, Ernesto Miranda was arrested in Arizona for kidnapping and rape. After a two-hour interrogation, Miranda, who had a history of mental instability, signed a confession that was used against him at trial. His court-appointed attorney objected, arguing that the police had not informed Miranda of his rights to counsel and to remain silent, making the confession less than voluntary. The objection was overruled, and Miranda was found guilty.

The Arizona Supreme Court affirmed the decision, but the U.S. Supreme Court voted 5–4 against allowing the confession into evidence. It held that statements made by a defendant in response to police interrogation are admissible only if the defendant was informed of his rights prior to questioning. It found Miranda a particularly vulnerable interviewee, due to his schizophrenic illness.

Miranda was retried in 1967 and convicted without the prosecution's use of the confession. He was paroled in 1972, but was in and out of prison over the next several years for various offenses. While free, he made a modest living working odd jobs and selling autographed Miranda Warning cards on the steps of the Phoenix courthouse. He was stabbed to death in a fight in 1976. Several Miranda cards were found on him.

81

Material Demonstration Documents Testimony

Common categories of evidence

Judge: "Am I never to hear the truth?"

Counsel: "No, my lord, merely the
evidence."

—PETER MURPHY,
A Practical Approach to Evidence,
3rd Edition (1988)

Johnnie Cochran, criminal defense attorney

The integrity of the system is more important than the truth of one case.

A trial's search for truth is invariably imperfect, because it cannot be conducted in a way that introduces unfair methods into the legal system. If a piece of evidence was improperly acquired or mishandled by the prosecution, it may be excluded from trial even if it provides an incontrovertible link between the defendant and the crime, because evidence in all future cases could be similarly abused. If this allows a guilty person to go free, it isn't because the court is disinterested in the truth of the case; it is because it accepts that the truth sometimes must suffer in the short run so the court gets better at finding the truth in the long run.

83

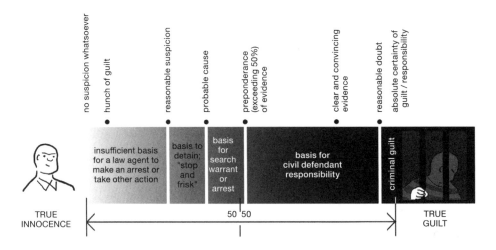

no suspicion whatsoever

hunch of guilt

reasonable suspicion

probable cause

preponderance (exceeding 50%) of evidence

clear and convincing evidence

reasonable doubt

absolute certainty of guilt / responsibility

insufficient basis for a law agent to make an arrest or take other action

basis to detain; "stop and frisk"

basis for search warrant or arrest

basis for civil defendant responsibility

criminal guilt

TRUE INNOCENCE

50 50

TRUE GUILT

Standards of proof

A jury that believes a criminal defendant is "probably guilty" must acquit.

In issuing a verdict of guilty, a jury asserts its belief, beyond a reasonable doubt, that a criminal defendant is responsible for a crime. Such doubt must be derived rationally from the evidence, or from a lack of evidence, presented by the prosecution. It cannot be based on sympathy for the accused or on fanciful conjecture, such as whether a time traveler was the true perpetrator of the crime.

84

A judge trial might better suit:

- a case with complex legal questions
- a pro se (self-represented) litigant, as a judge might know to disregard irrelevant/ inflammatory evidence
- a large organization opposing a small organization or individual

A jury trial might better suit:

- a litigant whose case has a strong emotional component
- a personal injury litigant
- an individual or small organization opposing a large organization

A guilty verdict isn't binding.

A verdict is a jury's decision as to whether the facts presented to it fit the essential elements of a crime or civil harm. The judge uses the verdict as a guideline in creating an appropriate final judgment. A judge must accept a verdict of not guilty, but in most jurisdictions the court may set aside all other civil and criminal verdicts if it determines that the jury reached its verdict in error or did not base it on sufficient evidentiary ground.

85

Objection, irrelevant.

The answer won't tend to prove or disprove a fact.

Objection, prejudicial.

The answer will mislead or confuse the jury.

Objection, no foundation.

This witness lacks firsthand knowledge of the matter.

Objection, privileged.

My client does not have to reveal the confidences of her spouse.

Objection, hearsay.

The person to whom these remarks are attrbuted is not on the witness list.

Common objections

The battle might not be worth the collateral damage.

Every case involves many small points of dispute, such as courtroom procedures, the admissibility of evidence, or an inaccurate assertion by the opponent that, if refuted, may leave the jury confused. Winning cases often lose some of these battles. Size up quickly if a battle is worth fighting or if you should move on. Picking too many battles can undermine your credibility before the court, and losing unnecessary disputes may boost the confidence of your opponent and reduce the likelihood of a desired settlement.

If a point of dispute is not central to your theory of the case, it likely will not work in your favor to engage it. But if overruled on a crucial matter, request that your objection be put on the record in case you lose the case and need to appeal the decision.

86

Roe v. Wade, 410 U.S. 113 (1973)

Norma McCorvey, unsuccessful in her efforts to obtain an illegal abortion in Texas, sued the State of Texas in federal court. She claimed that state laws restricting abortion violated her right to privacy. The court ruled in favor of McCorvey (who used the alias "Jane Roe"), but declined to issue an injunction that would have lifted the abortion ban.

On appeal by Roe, the U.S. Supreme Court, acting simultaneously on the companion case of *Doe v. Bolton*, ruled that the Constitution creates a right to personal privacy that extends to a woman's decision to have an abortion. However, the Court balanced this right against the state's interest in guarding prenatal life and women's health by limiting state regulation to the third trimester of pregnancy. The Supreme Court later revised this limit to the point of fetal viability.

Roe v. Wade was a case of won battles and lost wars, or vice versa. Roe gave birth before the first trial was complete. She won her case in district court but was not granted the injunction she desired. But the district court nonetheless helped Roe fight a larger cause: its decision left room for the U.S. Supreme Court to issue a ruling with farther-reaching force that affected all the states. In later decades, McCorvey came to regret her role in *Roe v. Wade* and became a pro-life advocate.

87

	Vote in case favored Bush (Republican)	Vote in case favored Gore (Democrat)
Justices nominated by a Republican President		
Rehnquist	✓	
Scalia	✓	
Thomas	✓	
O'Connor	✓	
Kennedy	✓	
Souter		✓
Stevens		✓
Justices nominated by a Democratic President		
Ginsburg		✓
Breyer		✓

U.S. Supreme Court Justices in *Bush v. Gore*, 531 U.S. 98 (2000)

Judges are biased.

Judges and juries interpret facts through the lenses of their own experiences. Although they may strive to be impartial, they cannot be completely aware of or completely put aside their biases.

88

"We are under a Constitution, but the Constitution is what judges say it is."

—CHARLES EVANS HUGHES,
U.S. Supreme Court Associate Justice (1910–1916)
and Chief Justice (1930–1941)

89

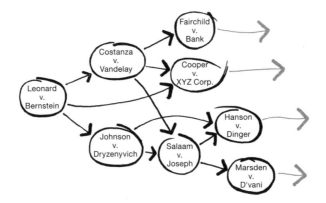

A legal ruling is the beginning, not the end, of the life of the law.

A court decision may conclude a given case, but it is likely to affect a line of cases far into the future. **Stare decisis**—the requirement that each court stand by previous decisions made by it, and by higher courts in its jurisdiction—ensures that the law is predictable, that similar acts are adjudicated similarly, and that the consequences of a given action are known.

90

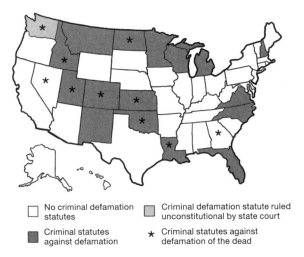

☐ No criminal defamation statutes	☐ Criminal defamation statute ruled unconstitutional by state court
■ Criminal statutes against defamation	＊ Criminal statutes against defamation of the dead

States deliberately pass unconstitutional laws.

Many outdated state statutes, such as those criminalizing sodomy and defamation, remain on the books in the United States despite having been declared unconstitutional by the U.S. Supreme Court. A conviction made under them in state court likely would be overturned if appealed to the U.S. Supreme Court.

States sometimes pass **trigger laws** to express disagreement with the U.S. Supreme Court's interpretation of the Constitution. Such laws have a provision stating they will take effect (be triggered) if the Supreme Court changes its interpretation of the Constitution. A number of states have passed trigger laws to abolish abortion in the event that the U.S. Supreme Court overturns its 1973 decision in *Roe v. Wade*.

91

Photos of possible perpetrators shown one at a time instead of in groups, to discourage selection through elimination

Photo IDs conducted by computer or by police officers unfamiliar with the case to minimize suggestion

Witness informed that none of individuals viewed may be the perpetrator, to discourage selection of "most likely"

Some recent reforms in eyewitness identification

Memory is a crime scene.

According to the Innocence Project, more than three-fourths of convicts exonerated by DNA testing had been found guilty on the basis of eyewitness testimony. Once thought highly accurate, eyewitness memory of an event is now known to be distorted by subsequent events, including the manner in which police conduct questioning, photo identifications, and lineups. Like an unprotected crime scene, one's memory of a crime is a record that can be irrevocably altered by later events taking place in the same space.

Ronald Cotton and Jennifer Thompson

Ronald Cotton exoneration

Jennifer Thompson, a white college student, was attacked in her bed by an intruder. She carefully studied the rapist's features, and in a later photo lineup identified Ronald Cotton, an African American, as her attacker. Cotton lacked a convincing alibi, and was tried and convicted. He received a life sentence.

In prison, Cotton crossed paths with inmate Bobby Poole, to whom he bore a resemblance; guards and other inmates occasionally confused the two. Poole bragged that he had committed the crime for which Cotton had been convicted. Cotton gained a retrial, but Thompson again identified him as her attacker and did not recognize Poole, who was in the courtroom. Convicted of the Thompson rape again, as well as another rape also based on eyewitness identification, Cotton received a new sentence of life plus 54 years.

Back in prison, Cotton contemplated killing Poole, who lived in the same dormitory, but was talked out of it by his father. Seven years after his second conviction, new lawyers for Cotton requested review of the DNA evidence. The only sample left was the partial head of a sperm. But it was enough to prove conclusively that Poole was the rapist. Ronald Cotton was freed after serving 10.5 years. Poole later died in prison.

Two years after Cotton's release, he and Thompson met and became close friends. They wrote a bestselling book about their experiences, and campaign together for reform in eyewitness testimony.

"We don't see things as they are,
but as we are."

—ANAÏS NIN

Retributive justice

focuses on satisfying the
victim and community by meting
out punishment in proportion to
the crime, the damage done, or
the benefit gained by the offender

Restorative or reparative justice

focuses holistically on the needs
of victims, the community, and
offenders, who are asked to
acknowledge, take responsibility
for, and repair harms

People act from a center of pain.

When in conflict, people rarely act from a rational, logical center. Otherwise reasonable individuals may distort the truth and lash out in anger due to fear, rejection, and frustration over being misunderstood, while attributing their upset to other factors. Often, conflicts can be resolved without litigation, by making sure each party fully hears the other side and is fully heard itself, without interruption. People will usually live with disagreement when they are certain they have been heard and understood, and will often forgive wrongs when they know the reasons for them.

There never was a Twinkie defense.

San Francisco city supervisor Dan White, by many accounts, was a conscientious, respected member of his community. But in 1978, several days after resigning his position, White entered City Hall through an unguarded window and murdered supervisor Harvey Milk and Mayor George Moscone. White's defense team did not deny he committed the crime, but claimed he had been severely depressed and suffered from diminished mental capacity, making him incapable of the premeditation required for first-degree murder. A psychiatrist testified to the symptoms of White's depression, including a switch from a healthy diet to one full of sugary snacks. The jury agreed that White's capacity was diminished, and convicted him of voluntary manslaughter. He received a seven-year sentence.

A tumultuous aftermath included public demonstrations and rioting, and the eventual abolition of the diminished capacity defense in California. A sarcastic reporter referred to White's defense as the "Twinkie defense." The phrase stuck, and it is still used to refer to an improbable or highly suspect defense tactic. However, no argument was made by White's lawyers that his diet caused him to commit the murders, only that it evidenced his depression.

96

"If only there were evil people somewhere insidiously committing evil deeds, and it were necessary only to separate them from the rest of us and destroy them. But the line dividing good and evil cuts through the heart of every human being. And who is willing to destroy a piece of his own heart?"

—ALEKSANDR SOLZHENITSYN,
The Gulag Archipelago (1973)

97

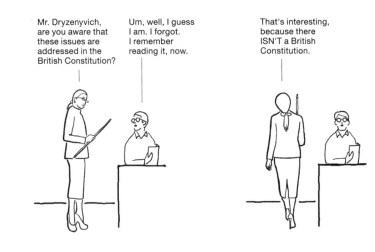

The other students are scared, too.

Law school is tough for everyone, and law professors are often demanding and unclear. Owning your ignorance and asking questions are among your best tools for survival. The best questions to ask are often those you fear will make you appear stupid; the likelihood is high that other students will have the same questions. And, perhaps as important, speaking up in class is good practice for speaking up in court.

Insurance   Family   Land use

Sports   Arts   Marine

Most areas of law interest have a corresponding area of law practice.

Law is a profession of specialties. Attorneys work in diverse fields, including medical, sports, family, art, drug control, environment, Native American, prison, media, and dozens more.

99

You have to *find* a mentor; no one is going to make you a protégé.

It is unlikely anyone will seek you out to nurture your career, no matter how talented you are. Although many organizations have formal mentoring programs, a long-term mentor is usually someone you connect with over time on an intellectual and personal level.

   You probably will have to do most of the work. Ask questions of those around you. Most people like to be asked for advice. Don't worry about their stature; a low-ranking associate could soon be a partner. But make your requests manageable; ask for input on specific issues. Save broad questions of career and legal philosophy for after hours.

Hillary Clinton

A career in law is continual preparation for a day that may never come.

Everything a lawyer does must be done with awareness of how it will hold up in a trial. Yet lawyers rarely get to argue in court. Even professional litigators spend little time in the courtroom, as over 90% of both criminal and civil cases are resolved prior to trial by plea bargain or settlement. Many suits are filed not with the goal of going to trial, but to prompt settlement by the other party.

A lawyer can't merely love being a performer, but must love the law.

101

Index

Vibeke Norgaard Martin is an attorney in Carmel-by-the-Sea, California, where she primarily practices municipal law. Previously, she practiced extensively in both commercial and civil rights litigation. She has taught at the Boalt School of Law at the University of California, Berkeley, was a visiting scholar at the Centre for Child Law at the University of Pretoria in South Africa, worked for the Sierra Leone Truth and Reconciliation Commission, and clerked for the South African Constitutional Court.

Matthew Frederick is an architect, urban designer, instructor of design and writing, and the creator of the acclaimed 101 Things I Learned series. He lives in New York's Hudson Valley.